The Shape of a Throat

The Shape of a Throat

Sheila Stewart

Clarise Foster, Editor

Signature
EDITIONS

Cover design by Doowah Design.
Photo of Sheila Stewart by Liz Szynkowski.

Printed and bound in Canada.

We acknowledge the support of The Canada Council for the Arts and the Manitoba Arts Council for our publishing program.

Acknowledgements
Poems from this collection have appeared in *ARC, Canadian Woman Studies, Contemporary Verse 2, dANDelion, Descant, Grain, Misunderstandings Magazine, Our Times, qwerty, The Literary Review of Canada, The New Quarterly, The Toronto Quarterly, White Wall Review, Windsor Review*, and on-line in *Branch, Educational Insights and LEARNing Landscapes.*

A big thank you to Karen Haughian and everyone at Signature Editions. Thank you to Clarise Foster, my editor, for careful, thoughtful attention.

Thank you to Barry Dempster for fine editing and helping to bring this manuscript toward a book. Thank you to Karen Solie and everyone at the Banff Wired Writing Studio 2005. Thank you to writing friends whose feedback on the manuscript helped it find its way: Elizabeth Greene, Ruth Roach Pierson, Betsy Trumpener, and Liz Ukrainetz. Thank you to The Long Dash members who commented on the poems: Clara Blackwood, Merle Nudelman, John Oughton, Mary Lou Soutar-Hynes, and Elana Wolff. Thank you to Guy Ewing, Maureen Hynes, Libby Shea, and Leela Viswanathan. Thank you to Marianne Apostilides for walking. Thank you to Bhasker and Margaret Pathak for encouragement. Thank you to Ardra Cole, Nancy Jackson, and Lorri Neilsen Glenn for how this inquiry unfolds into the next.

I am grateful for the support of the Toronto Arts Council.

Library and Archives Canada Cataloguing in Publication

Stewart, Sheila

The shape of a throat / Sheila Stewart.

Poems.

ISBN 978-1897109-95-3

I. Title.

PS8587.T4896S53 2012 C811'.6 C2012-901732-9

Signature Editions
P.O. Box 206, RPO Corydon, Winnipeg, Manitoba, R3M 3S7
www.signature-editions.com

for Richard
Rachel and Maya

Contents

In the beginning

word leapt from body
and never returned. Body said, *you're mine.*
Word said, *I'm free.* Page waited patiently,
knew word would want to lie down in time, would
fall in love with crisp white sheets, with making a mark.
Edge along the page, and lie
still.

Falling through me

China teacup

            boiling water poured
the bottom fell right out

I can't be filled

                    experience
falls through me

I leave this world
                    the bottom
                            drops

a teacup that can't
            hold tea
                    throw it out

            says a voice

fling into the garden
            a broken pot

                              tipped
trapped
            in soil's cloying squelch
shoots and roots growing
            through the shards

in the garden of buried teacups
            bones   a cat's skeleton
                        the sharp tiny teeth
of a rabbit

what is metaphor   the shape
            of a throat

The call

Casting, conjuration, words wanting
air, mouth round. Paper fraudulent.

Late slips, bad news, bad cheque.
Some nouns are kisses, wanting

all of you. What the tongue can do,
lips pursed and puckered. Words

like willows. Verbs won't make it better.
All we have uttered, will utter.

Announce.

It matters

how you enter — when, where, why, with whom.
Once you came here in a short green dress with your husband, walked

the edge of the lake at dusk. Ten years before children.
In August the goldenrod starts to flower — soon it will wash the park

in mustard. Later this park will whiten. Once you sat in the café,
tabletop embossed with leaves, noticed the tree, window-framed,

arms outstretched. Couldn't speak it. Black oak bent, branches
thick as its trunk. Now you've found the tree, run to it, run

your hand over rivulets of rough bark.
What to offer?

Brush, scrape, the sound of friction

— it matters.

Two black oaks

growing on a hill
one with a hole where a limb was severed
trunk bent at the hips
the other leaning   into its heels
struggling on the incline

tired some days with sheltering

what is sorrow for
but to lie down in
where is happiness   oh, to lie down
back burrowed into oak
nestled into memory
a hand
pressing the small of my back

A broken sugar maple

stands exposed at the side of Spring Road.
Hit by lightning, a storm like an enraged father. A thick
severed branch pressed into the soil. Pale wood juts upright,

sinuous belly, exposed to light, the elements. It wants
the thin cloak of bark, rings chewed up by the fall,
spat out. Bearing the pain of the phantom limb.

My friend takes photographs of willows bending towards a pond,
the red bark of Austrian pine, bulbous burls. I dream the fractured
flesh of maple filling the frame of my vision: no characters, chase,

obstacles. No battle, dialogue. Where is diversion when I need it?
We can't help but storytell. Sitting on a worn oak chair in a café
listening to jazz, arms resting on a pine table. Even the ceiling pine,

knots gazing down. I want a tall maple to shade me. I'm left
gazing at a picture of light falling through a forest,
as if that's all I need.

You must cross the big road

to enter the park, trucks trundling
to the expressway. Lift up your small white dog, step into the road.
A bench faces the woods. Chickadees flit through dogwood.

Someone has been here, left you a star
of elm leaves. A collection of yellow ash, circle of mushrooms, sumac's
velvet cones carefully arranged where paths cross.

The trees have split their bark. They try
to shed it, break through. It can't contain them. The sound of chickadees,
then sirens. First time you've heard them here.

The allotments have been
allotted. You have your dog. A chickadee lands at your feet, another on
your shoulder, black cap close to your own. They light on your hand, can't
believe it is empty.

You walk through
the park carrying a notebook, uncomfortable with it out in plain view.
Rustle dead leaves, stare a squirrel in the eye. No food for it either.

Everything wants to fill
its cheeks. Gather, store. A man stuffs a bag, compost or oak leaves.
Leans into it. All paths intersect. Flame trees over the hill.

Dogs run at each other,
eager to sniff. Log across a trail. Vine climbing oak. An empty
shopping cart at park's edge. You take a route you don't know. Turned
around, you emerge at a road you thought was elsewhere.

It doesn't matter who you love but how,
how you hold the small flutter in your palm, offer it to them, hand
outstretched.

It is autumn, mid afternoon, the children
still in school.

Alone for the weekend

I forgot to put my skin on. I blow
about the streets, a scrap of page.
I sit in the window of the public
library, unbound.

An old man strokes his beard
at the next table. I should be safely
home with daffodils.

Yellow cups.

Frills.

How you take

the subway, your chest cut
down the middle, heart awake, exposed —
going somewhere, a job, a deadline, focus, skin

turned inside out. Eyes
closed. What do they see? Around you people
are sleeping and

you have forgotten how.

Making room

In the park the sky lifts, making room for my midwinter steps, dog gazing at the distance. I can only write poems to people I know. I don't want to be a burden to anyone. Sky and snow everywhere, bare limbs of soaked trees exposed.

Early February small murmurs and growls far away within the earth, one voice stretching toward another. You, longing to write, what do you want to say? Is it patience — how the weather shifts?

Make room for our hands, what is outside the window, what weighs heavy, what lifts us like the sun warming the backs of our heads as we walk — all the while considering the dog's constant sniffing. The poem sometimes endless, sometimes portal.

So much depends

                    on a way to enter water, lie across the top, catching
waves, rocked from side to side. Let water flow, surround. The dock's

weathered wood sand-colour. Perpendicular marker. Spring to Thanksgiving,
a place to sit, dangle feet into the lake, tether boats. Washed, buoyed, taken.

A way to stand on water. We can't find our footing, are rarely elegant on earth.
The lake bathes our misgivings, slips between our toes, caresses our ankles,

baptizes us in the names of our daughters. Careens, whispers, croons.
Call of the loon lifting. All we can do.

Water

rushes in rapids

smooth back hips cheeks
rock-face

cascades
wants to speak

ragged stones

quartz marble granite sand
neither lapping nor storming

resting between shores
fill pour overflow

water can lift a rock hurl
at the shore
reach and reach

as if rock sees and longs
as if it can raise itself
tumble into water
home

Between you and the sky

There's nothing between you and sky. Your parents dead. You need something, even an umbrella, a hat. What would protect you? You just keep looking around, thinking about things. One parent disappeared, you still had the other. Until he died over breakfast. You look out the front window, people walking by, old people too, breathing beautifully. Last week you walked out the door, went to work. Not an umbrella in sight. Distance only distance, tucked behind houses.

Poetry is a theory

of everything, the smell of ginger root, roasting garlic, crushed cardamom, the taste of nutmeg, the trouble with memory, a writer's unreliability, the lie of the lake. Five needle clusters on the white pine, two on the red.

The way I can look you in the eye, let meaning go. Try not to call it anything at all. Hope. Capture a moth under a glass, release it. Words standing in as best they can, bravely, not knowing they come up short. They try their best, like the rest of us.

Poetry is not giving up on each other, coming back, surprised we are still here. Sometimes, even young.

Poetry is the speed of light, entering a lake midsummer, you swimming toward me, swinging me through the waves we both make. I dive off your shoulders, porpoise between your legs. We are conjunctions, prepositions. Verbs tensed in pleasure.

Water keeps approaching relentlessly, crests in time to meet sand, redemption — resolution. The perfect pitch of a long shoreline, stones washed bright. How I can't tell yours from my own.

The other side of the page

Between body and

> Setting foot on the middle ground
> between body and word, which contains,
> or is supposed to, other
> people.
>
> Margaret Atwood, from "You Come Back"

stepping into lilacs after writing,
remembering this stunning spring
a whole summer
and more

between body and word —
a slipper, a big English penny
from 1939, my father's sermon,
sadness, a handwritten report card,
"Sheila is easily frustrated."
One of the year's standard comments?
Was the teacher easily frustrated
or

in between, beside, behind,
under dandelion leaves,
below radar, on the top
bunk, behind the chimney
sweep, within

people,
who walk around as if everything
is normal, as if they could
forever, as if *setting foot on*
the middle ground between body
and word,
which contains.

When no one is looking

Lift the floral sugar-bowl lid, fingers
round the silver-clawed tongs. Squeeze
a cube. Place it in the centre of
your palm. Raise it to your

tongue. Step away from the bowl, look
out the window into the neighbours' yard:
      snow falling on their red swing set.
            Suck slow. Melt.

All quiet? Check that the grown-ups
are still busy.

            Again.

My father reading

the newspaper
no trespassing

he's tired and has a meeting
disturbed he scowls
hulking

hallowed kingdom
the lake shines blue

thy will be done   every
one knows my father
the adults line up in the narthex
after the sermon to shake his hand

if I line up there too
will he

want to see me
reach for my fingers

Sunday morning

The sermon was too long, a wearing
down. What did the congregation think
about? Hear? Mr. Pounder listened like

it was meant for him, shook my father's hand.
Mrs. Thrasher and the woman she sat beside
whispered, *thank you* — he understood.

My father's words sprinkled among his flock,
while we waited, parched, gulping thin air.
We could have plunged our heads into stagnant

baptismal water, spewed it over the altar,
drowning God.

Do I write

because of the word of God.
All we Presbyterians have is an empty cross.
So open-minded, all symbolism and parable,
the love of neighbour and community. We eat
the sign of Christ's body, broken for us,
drink the image of his blood spilled for us,
and plan the next potluck supper on the back
of an envelope.

Father worked extra at holidays

From the pulpit, *Christmas is ruined by the sin*
of commercialism. Some of you won't be back

until next Christmas. The packed pew shuffled,
looked away. *Special services for those lazy hypocritical people*

who only darken the door of the church at Christmas and Easter.
Weddings and baptisms. Call themselves Christian.

We were thanked with boxes of chocolates — Black Magic
— the spongy paper guide to plain chocolates, hazelnut crunch.

Beware the sticky soft cherry ones. Hampers of goodies,
strawberry jams and apricot squares. Wives, mothers up late

cutting out shortbread, women working to keep Father happy.

After

Curls of red, brown, yellow pool at our feet.
A trunk with a gaping hole like the one

they made in my mother's chest. Worked
on her heart as if it was their own.

When she woke, I was far away
in the wrong smell of another family.

My father couldn't look
after a little girl, who

couldn't look after
herself.

Learning the alphabet

I'd always known
the letter T, the lines on my mother's chest, one across, another down
between her breasts. A Roman cross. T for Turtle, Trunk, Time, Taste,

Trust. Never mentioned it, never touched it. "No," she said, "I can't wear
a neckline that low." My chest is uncut, skin intact. My children have all
their limbs. The tiny suture on the last-born is a faint thread.

"Inguinal hernia," they said. "Better safe than sorry." The most recent:
a squiggle above her eye, stitches from a slam against a window.
We watch each other, my generation. What are the signs? Quiver

at the neck. A bit thinner. Talking, Truth, Touch. How do we keep each
other alive? Look back at the seniors' home and my great-aunt is waving.
She waits to hear if they'll operate. Her thin arms score the window.

We believe

We are mad for monuments. Ruins, stadiums, stone walls, statues, tombs, forts, fortresses. Tell us the size, weight, height, the amount of gold. Give us the numbers of people, the years to build them.

Tell us of slaves, rulers, battles, people who died young, heroes, beautiful wives who waited, ships in full sail. It's what we want to hear, we believe it, this is why we have come. We've been somewhere and we must be the better for it. My, what we have learned.

We don hats and walking shoes, carry water and sunscreen. Learn *hello, please, thank you* in the local language. Take another photograph. Buy postcards. Fridge magnets.

Sugar

1.

Dust rises off the hot low veldt. Vast sugarcane estates: the only irrigated land. Wide lush green fields sprout a million tiny sprinklers. The cane is ready, burnt to make it easier to cut. Flame sweeps the fields, fierce as a forest fire. The air black soot, a flurry of ash falls miles away, drifts in doorways, a line of soot runs across the table in our classroom Monday morning, mirroring the crack in the roof's peak.

2.

How I love a dusting of sugar over a slab of chocolate cake, a script of raspberry sauce.

3.

Give me brown sugar, white sugar, cubes and icing sugar, caster sugar, sugar daddy, sugar mummy, sugar baby, sugar bear, sugar beet, sugar bowl, sugared and sugary, sugar plum fairy, *Shake Sugaree.*

4.

Long, open cane trucks, chains along the sides, drive past the auto-wreck's *Jesus is Coming,* into the refugee settlement, collect workers early in the morning, return them dirty, tired at day's end. The cane cutters earn a little more, dressed in layers for protection, sooty as chimney sweeps. Our students tell us, *Cane can cut you. Snake can get you in the cane.*

5.

Monthly rations: maize, beans, salt, sometimes dried fish, and a little sugar.

6.

One more lump of sugar, please.

7.

Simon learned English fast: *homeland, refugee, truck. Hot and cold. Love and hate. Past, present, future.* Simon cut cane. He told us of his last trip on the back of a cane truck. Returning to the settlement one black night, the truck broke down at the side of the road. People got out, lay down and slept, waiting for another truck. Simon watched a lorry full of oranges crash into the cane truck, knocking it over onto the sleeping workers, pinning the dead and injured to the ground. The sugary smell of oranges but none to eat. The truck carried on, cutting through the night, taking the oranges safely to Durban.

Shy in Greece

The birds are shy in Greece, he says on our second day. Twenty years later
we are here again — this time with children. The last day, *do you want to come*
with me to the mudflats to look for shorebirds? That morning I had said, *you give*

the kids more attention than you give me. Nights in Napflion we walk
the boardwalk, sea crashing against rocks, our near-teenage children
screaming as they're sprayed. We stand on the pier, arms open

to the sea, wanting the push of wind. Blue-black clouds. Should I tell you
about the swastikas spray-painted on the rocks? In Toronto we wash walls
and rocks. The mudflats are near a train track on the edge of industry.

Larks and pipits sit atop gravel piles. I'm first to spot the Great Egret's flash
of white at the shore. Twenty years ago we were angry about the torture of
Central Americans. Now we avoid English-language papers and English-speaking

tourists. We climb hills to temples and ruins, fill our heads with Zeus, Athena,
Poseidon, Persephone — want to know if this bird is the female Crested Lark,
or a different species altogether. The egret lifts languorously, following the shore.

How do they find each other, he asks, handing me binoculars. A fleck of egret
coming into focus, settling with another.

The other side of the page

A house full of pages with one word changed. Turn them over
to big round heads with spider-like arms and legs sprawling.
All the crayon colours. Their drawings on

the backs of my poems. She sits at her child's table, covered in stickers,
by the kitchen window, stretching limbs to the page's edge. One day I'm
cutting carrots as usual and

fingers, toes arrive in ones and twos. Mathematics
of exact numbers. One word fewer. Or more.
A change of order. New place to start. *Look, Daddy as a baby.*

The curved and straight lines of mouths: she sees who smiles and frowns.
Do I break the line? *You're here, Mummy, buying apples.*
She points to the left

beyond the page's border.

Parental guidance

1.

Daughters eating Shreddies, brimming with questions. Turn the radio off quick. Don't leave it on and go upstairs. They'll be up after you, asking you to explain *human remains*.

2.

Newspapers are better, but check the front-page photo before you leave it lying about. Read out the good stories over breakfast. Show the girls the picture of Marg and the pigeons, how Marg carries scissors everywhere to cure their Stringfoot, snips from between their toes human hair, string, wire and monofilament fishing line, debris which hobbles them, cuts off their circulation. She squirts electrolyte formula into the mouths of the dehydrated, does a world of good.

3.

Pour their orange juice, hope for the best.

Backfloat

                                          across Emma Lake,
gazing up into a blue bowl rimmed in pine.
I'm kicking slowly. Christine and Matthew

are separating. The news ripples
through us. We stare at our children,
today's photo album intact.

We watch each other, tend our couplings
like orchids, careful watering, turning
the buds toward

                                          the light. All that sky.
What lies on the other side of the water.

When my daughter plays the piano

I think she is talking
to me — a language of scales and chords I don't know. Presence
and grace. Thursdays after school, I walked slowly to Mr. Scott's

house, hoped Mrs. Scott would be there too. He was the organist,
his name on the church sign alongside my father's. Choir practice
was easier: he didn't notice me. Thursdays he pushed my fingers

into the keys, broke pencils. Red rushed from his neck
to his white hair: I without talent, I didn't practice.
Six months later we moved. No piano in the new manse.

When my daughter plays, I stop — listen. My throat fills.
I've been busy practising, being her mother: *eat your breakfast.*
How was your day? I don't know the notes to reach for.

In concert

Notes written up the back of the cellist's hand, fathers and mothers sitting on hard chairs in the hot school auditorium, children's smooth faces before us. Big band tunes, glints of brass. I change seats to better see my fourteen-year-old daughter, to watch her stare above sheets of music, eyes on the conductor. I'm glad she chose French horn rather than the clarinet, my grade eight instrument.

The other day I cycled past a music store, glimpsed a row of clarinets, hanging like trophies: keys bright. My father had said, *I will get you one for Christmas if you promise to practise, if it won't sit in the case, if you are serious.* I pedaled back, looked in the window, but couldn't go into the store. I wanted him to give me what I wanted.

In transit

Thule

As if you are rising towards me
suspended in a glass case.
You lie still. Big paintings, massive
birdmen and shards of mirror shouting

the twentieth century around us.
Tiny female, date unknown,
your hands clasped
at your stomach. Relic,

like the mismatched miniatures
my friend Nora and I played with.
We called them Knickerbocker Newbies,
each of us arriving with our box of

animals and dolls — hers had a thimble,
mine a two-inch chair. All different
smallnesses, the horse smaller than frog.
How we marched them about the sofa,

knelt on the floor as they visited, traveled,
catapulted. Oh, to take them out of the box,
set them on couch or carpet. Like the lights
dimming at the movie theatre before

Mary Poppins, the lion on the big screen growling
something-very-exciting-is-about-to-begin.
Or, the thick curtain parting on a fully furnished
room, lights on, the woman begins to speak.

Knickerbocker Newbies was our real game,
better than Fish or Clue, even Kick the Can.
I was the youngest — never understood
the big kids' games, brothers' rules.

Dusk running between the hedges,
under the bushes, the places
where our yard met the neighbours',
secret corners, thrill meets fear, lost

between the houses out back. May I
call you *Thule,* after your birthplace?
Who carved you, feminine statue older
than Eve? Chiseled your limbs,

smoothed your brow, enfolded you
in their palm. Face obscured, dark nipples.
Your arms so short, fingers just touch
over your belly. Could they protect you?

Legs tight together. Child. Amulet,
talisman. How you raced through
the hedgeless terrain, hill's ledge, thin
line of the stream. Didn't need to ask

which way to run.

In transit

Stand at the window, front of the first car, end of the last. Be a child, run to the window, gaze down the long tunnel. Look away from the other passengers and grip the metal pole.

Once streetcars had high ceilings, open sides, conductors made change, walked along the ledge. Then the motorcar came, conductors fell in its path. The sides were closed in. Now crammed in humid stalls, we grip the rails, pretend to be alone. Never knowing how close to get.

Try to choose the best spot, the child's. Look out, try to be comfortable. Put your hand to your own. Curves and light. Lyric or narrative? Nothing to say for once. All our verbs spin ahead. Behind us, all the nouns we will ever need.

What can you do on the subway?

Read, read like mad, all the books in your bag,
read to your heart's content, books of the people

beside you — filling in the plot, marking their stops
so you can read them on their way back home.

Bible, Koran — pocket sized. *Metro* tabloid and ads for free.
The things we read because we can't help it. *Improve*

Your Sex Life… the road to success… up to 50% more…
is the future in your hands? Bright as sailboats, draining

the colour from flesh. The person you've been thinking about,
want to avoid. A train full of people who shower, some sing.

Before me — the perfect face of a stranger. As if this car holds
an answer. Poses a question. You can write a poem — cover it

with your hand when it arouses suspicion. Learn a foreign language,
eavesdrop.

The 506 streetcar

                                        pushes through
the Red Sea of the city. Angela's Coin
Laundry Open 7 Days a Week, New Dryers

Sam and Nick Barber Shop
Shalom Evangelical Bookstore
Blvd. of Broken Seams receding

as the streetcar weaves west. Curious
— it wants to know what's what, to finger
sleeves in dress stores, sip espresso, eat

at Grappa. Grilled calamari, smoked salmon,
a carafe of red wine. Farther west
Pho Linh Fine Vietnamese Cuisine.

Psychic Florence speaks Italian, Portuguese
Spanish. Helps in All Problems in Life.
Fresh Like Flowers Dry Cleaners.

                                        Up the hill,
over the bridge, gazing down
at the train tracks below.

                                        High Park
— a pair of lovers
                                        in the brush.

Underground

So many of us, our coats full of rain. I squeeze between a man and woman. We cough — stare straight ahead.

Double your skin moisture ..... She is naked, flawless, smooth — white legs, thighs. Her hair falls around her. Seated in a way that hides, displays. A slim man sits beneath her, head shaved. *Love your body,* says the ad.

When the woman beside me leaves, I shift to her spot, hoping not to seem rude. No one notices *Please do not block the doorway.* We are mid-tunnel, between work and home. We have forgotten that we've brought the rain underground.

Rush hour on the Bloor Line

To —

We're all thicker in coats and scarves. Stuck between *Palm Pilot, Gameboy* and *Tax Relief Annuities.* Lock eyes with the man in the ad. Across the car two women read: *Awake! Our Kingdom Come.* Who am I to speculate? The ad-man glares.

What was it like to travel by horse? Talk
                    to her. Guide her
                            by name.

From —

                    Rocked right up against each other. *My fiancé*
was electrocuted at work. How safe is your job? We are as far beneath
ground as we can go and still

                    be alive. *Feeling violated? Virgin Mobile Phones*
No Hidden Fees.

                    Soft faces ageing between stops.

Greenwood

Christine gathers branches on her front path.
Look, she points, *green wood, Greenwood, so next time you can find*

my stop. I've been walking these streets as if in a foreign city —
went too far, turned the wrong way, though I've been to her house

many times, can't cross the city, should have stayed home.
She's set out teacups, a *new tea set just right for this kind of conversation.*

Bees and strawberries scattered across white porcelain. Red berries, green
vines, buzz of yellow. Side by side on her kitchen couch. It's okay

to be late, even lost. Why should we know how to get from A to B?

Born

on the lip of winter, before dawn, you are
the steam inside the 504 streetcar, the breath

of all these people as the car moves down Roncesvalles
Grenadier to Pearson, my street to yours, your only

map your mother's arms and breasts, you are my breath
as I walk on a wet November night, step around the moving van

unloading on the sidewalk, *Moving to the Future* written across it,
you are your mother's hands squeezing mine, small fierce mouth

sucking my finger, splash of rain as I walk home early in the morning,
first to hold such small weight

We write facing the window

push our right hands across the pages,
don't interrupt, we can talk later. I try to ignore the café clatter, mothers

scolding toddlers: *We have all morning together. Can't we get along?*
A pair of old ladies walks past, one gesturing, her hands in a child's

striped mittens. Another time I sat opposite you. You waited. I started to talk:
There's so many ways to let them down. As my voice dipped, you leaned

toward me. Crow's feet around our eyes, lines at the corners of our mouths.
Our children have outgrown us. *Whose tippy cup? Whose hat? Hurry up.*

We are no longer mothers urging agreement. You ask, *You can't concentrate?*
The old woman's mittened hands in flight. Her friend inclines her head,

catching every word.

Most cafés have a big man

at a small table: *I always give her*
a great bonus at Christmas. $5000 this year. She's been with me
since the beginning. Voices murmur, rivering, till a word pops out

like a rock, stop, hit that one. The consoling smell of coffee and art.
It's quieter at home but so many drawers and papers lie in wait, eager
to interrupt. Email too — someone always needs help. Someone's

dying. You want another language, parts of speech trading places,
bleeding together: only sounds, no promises. Like a budgie
singing in its cage, squawking to be let out, though a voice will do.

I can't discard

my clothes at the back door,
walk into rain, let it fall on me, lie on the ground,

flatten into grass and old maple leaves.
Falling and angling, wetting the oak's

slabs and shingles of bark,
runnels on the window, streams.

I stay inside, dreaming of it,
reluctant to go out,

lonely
hearing

its soft peddle.

Houses

So many of them. What goes on inside? Real estate, investment, nest egg. You rattle round them, bang into prospective buyers on the stairs, in the hallway, at the kitchen table. Husband, kids, rabbit, birds, dog — your house cramped. Can you leave it behind? Moving frightens you. Noisy contractors clamour for space. Keep coming back, day after day, showing up at the door, sitting on the porch. Can't sleep in your bed, they're fixing the ceiling, your husband furious. He never noticed the ceiling. You email the agent. She's so friendly — you have no idea who she is. When you head into the dank basement, she says, "Shall I go first?" But why are you looking at this house full of hockey trophies and wicker baskets? *Monopoly, Scrabble, Risk.*

Selling the house

When she put up the sign, I was planting impatiens in the dark. *You're selling your house, right?* Her car trunk full of signs. She wiped one clean, polished it the way I had my dining table. (I took the cloth off, saw the mark my aunt said to clean with toothpaste.) Everything spacious and light, furniture crowded in the garage, a few props left to look like home.

When we saw this house, I noticed the map of the world on the kitchen bulletin board, the owner teaching her son to ride his bicycle in the back lane. His name on the sandbox, Ted, hooks at his height in the little room overlooking the yard. We sat on our neighbours' porch and watched a couple with a baby follow their agent up the steps.

Our agent said, *No, let the girls have their piano lesson at home, not a bad thing to hear a piano in a house.* We've emptied our memories into boxes, have nowhere to sit. We're our own stand-ins, making it all look like love.

We never made

love in the backyard
of our old house.
Could we
trespass now, go in through the back
gate, lie down where we
buried the rabbit, look back at this home,
wonder
what we did there —
my fingertips,
your palm.

A low moon talking

The maples appear the same as yesterday

                                        but they've been dreaming.
Saplings again, rehashed their squabble with squirrels, relived the advance of
an overbearing stand of beech, suffered an occasional logging nightmare.
Wake trembling, and not just the aspens. Dreaming their wood dreams.
Now, they stand untroubled, stalwart, yesterday's trials shed.

                                        The maples appear the same
as yesterday, but they've moved. Each midnight they take a step south.
By summer, they'll have reached the dock. If we sleep the sleep of babes,
they'll bend and dive. Their roots, like seaweed, trail behind them. Canoe
and rowboat will rock and rock.

Waking
a word

in my mouth like strange syllables clipped
— a word I can't pronounce, shape or hold.

We are soldiers fighting for our lives, planes approaching,
opening their bellies — hundreds of men in parachutes.

Slip to the dream before — a bush in our neighbour's tiny yard ensnares
our small white dog, burrs around her twisted face, one eye shut.

Fast forward: burial site or dump, a woman with her small white dog,
dead in her basket of papers and notes — is mine alive?

Everyone friendly and bohemian, Hornby Island midsummer.
Garbage recycled to art. Damn it, I've left
my children in the hot locked car, fat baby asleep.
Have I killed them? They
each other?

At our old house

the new couple
have a water problem. Each day the woman
spends two hours watering the garden

with a system of Tupperware containers and a wagon.
I suggest a hose coming out from the kitchen sink
through their lovely French doors we never had.

That's what we did, I say, annoying the man. I want
to leave their backyard but stand there staring.
Suddenly, we are in their living room, they are having

an interesting party I wasn't invited to. I try to leave
but the phone rings — it's for me. I can't hear
the voice. As I head for the door, the phone rings again —

this time I hear a woman trying to schedule me a meeting.
I must have agreed. Now a different man in the living room
talks about his writing so eagerly. It's as if they invited me.

The woman is happy enough, in a red flounced skirt.
I'm in their bedroom, ugly with their stuff. The windows
two vertical slits.

Everyone's father

has died at once. All my friends' fathers. Funerals
in all corners of the city. I'm at the Old Mill, a kind of funeral factory.

Teenage boys' arms hanging in their fathers' suits. I am reminded of
wedding parties mid-July in the manicured city parks. Which aunts,

bridesmaids are ours? Which pall-bearers, mourning sisters? I have met
Allison's cousins before, but we've all aged unrecognizably. Her father

made me ice cream cones after dinner. I'm to sing a solo —
but words in what order, a love song or grief.

Night thoughts

looking at three pairs of legs including my own leaning way up the wall
I lie between a pair of lovers
I scan their books piles rising to the ceiling
moon lifting outside the window
the woman says to the man *so aren't you staying?*
I want to slip away between her wanting
his reluctance

will you come visit me?

a poet I know has moved to a large house on Newfoundland's east coast
two big rooms one with a massive desk
she and her husband stoned children in the other room
a small photograph framed in a piece of bone
her grandmother's face instead of marrow

I'm pregnant with twins happy
a visiting friend queries
how can you possibly have twins at your age?
of course I've made a huge mistake
don't know how to explain a version of the rhythm method
based on the moon

my job ending crowding past the supervisor in a narrow entranceway
turn myself to the wall so a wide man entering
with a large parcel will not brush against the front of my body

will you come?

sitting in an empty church wanting to read arches space
moonlight through stained glass the custodian starts to vacuum
the carpet a baby raccoon runs behind a statue
a golden retriever sniffs at three dead mice snippets of matted fur
mangled the dog pokes his nose into them
the custodian will remove the bodies
my children won't see

I can't read my report card two Fs swim up
from the jumble of numbers words columns and rows charts and grids
two Fs French and
Failure

I imagine conversation choke on water I always imagine
a low moon talking *when will you come?*

Silver maple

The men are coming to cut the trees. Orange suits
and hard hats. Can I speak? They will start
with my towering silver maple, outside the kitchen
window, family of squirrels nesting mid-trunk.

Hibernation hole, eyes peek out. The city wants
to take down the old before they die, hydro wires
at risk. Silvery, ageing, flaking bark — but perfectly
sound. Saws whirring. Cut the legs out from under me.

They're liable to go for the young maple next.
The old woman *grew it from seed in a jar*. She squeezed
an English phrase from her Polish landscape. Moved
to less space with her sister; we moved to more, taking

over hers, the squirrels and trees oblivious. She planted it
on city property, infraction of a rule. Maple I meant to climb
chopped down. While they're at it, the lilacs her mother
gave her: their blooms distract drivers. I met her once, just

enough time to for her to mention her mother and the story
of the lilacs. I make up the rest. Lilacs shed on city land —
cut them down. They start on my silver maple, my hands
wet in the sink. Eyes on you, friend. Can't cut you down,

my protector: shade, shadow, shield.
                    State
I'm in.

            Cut us down

        (what can't be remembered
        known)

                    cart us away.

November 11th

In the library basement my yoga teacher
announces a few minutes of remembrance
— the whole building silent. I prefer
yoga's own silence.

My friend beside me leaving a lifetime's
teaching to write poetry — her last
Remembrance Day assembly. Final time
leading a straggle of children

into the auditorium. The principal talks
peace, but fills the students with Flanders Fields.
(I was good at standing still.) My friend tells me
of Nathan who screams in class as if a bayonet

pierces his side. She says to the children,
Have you ever been hurt? I have. She lets
them see her cry. The statue in the park
tells us courage is a man on horseback.

Grandfather returned from the war,
beat Gran. (My uncle told my brother told
me.) For the woman in the far corner
coming to yoga class is an act of courage —

leaving her room, combat. Stillness
on any ordinary day, an act
of remembering and not. *Let
your spine sink into the ground.*

Theory to practice

She can't read a word she's written,
manages to carry her work to the table, but can't
go further. Arms rest on paper, head drops, hair and

cheek fall to the first page. She dreams of horses charging —
thundering in her chest. She gazes at the white foaming
mouth of a stallion, becomes horse. All her dreams

line up, fold away. She wakes to bright
midday light — what can she remember?
She can't write, pen skirting paper. She can't

face words. Reluctantly she sews the elastic on her daughter's
first point shoes. Busy since her own childhood,
hardly a day off unless she counts maternity leaves.

Craving moments alone when her brain will stop repeating
what she said she said. Not all stories redeem. She will draw you
to her, kiss you — or, write *kissing*. Imagine her way into you.

A story

she steps into
her body travels through woods
gorge

lake water
push, pull, glide
most of her submerged
arc of her arm shoulder meets air
a swimmer buoyed
trailing a wake
water syllables:

water wants her
spring sun warming one side of her face
she forgets

a wardrobe where snow
is falling

When light comes

it is more than you remember, not just the house
across the street, recognizing it from the day before. The whole day
lit, in and around, over and under.

You can't escape day now.
If you trick yourself, you could still fall back asleep. There will be
time later to write. Take your good mind and focus, make pancakes,
the dog needs to be let in.

In brightness,
the children will shake off sleep, hungrily. In and around like words,
light moves, seeking angles and corners, wanting to touch and change
you, comfort you, tell you anything in the dark.

A towel could be
a shirt. A mouth, a mind. What does it mean to take another
into you? Back behind your pubic bone, under your ribs, a basin
for your heart.

You don't know how to be alone. With another.
You want to be held. Toast and notebook aren't enough. The birds
summon light from across the street. Parked cars emerge.

Your husband waking. Glass
of water. Chopin. Your children's voices, their own kind of light.

You need an empty house.

You can ignore the pets but not the people.
Always someone needing something
humans being human. You shut the door

yet how exuberantly they run up stairs,
talk on the phone. What kind of breakfast

do they eat without you? Will they forget
their gloves? They might wait outside your door
wanting tickets and slices of kiwi. Breathing

loudly. Don't want to disturb you, but
can't believe you aren't up.

Why would you
write in bed
when they have so much to say?

A poet I know

takes her manuscript
to bed
if there's no one
else there

I see her lolling about
gazing across the sheets languorously
closing her eyes
opening them so slowly

she flips through pages idly editing
a poem or two

I can't find my manuscript
let alone invite it
to my bed I can't hear a word it says
sound shape

my mother took to bed
with the *Reader's Digest*
airmail blues and *Chatelaine* resting
with her veined and gnarled legs

a poet I know
caresses the edge of each poem
rubs her nose along the first lines
slides the last poems between her lips

my mother grows big as I shrink
tucked in at her back neither poem nor
person can find me

my poems tell me
breathe in and out they lie with me until our breath matches
they turn my head toward the silver maple *see the crook in its limbs*
a tree at every window I am undone by their voices
feast upon it don't be afraid see what you can see

Arterial

1. Geometry

Layers of blue, orange and red, grid
of the London subway.
Paint runs down a canvas in its own deliberate

way — flows, meanders, falls.
Layer upon layer. Look at a painting,
under a colour.

Arriving home, you sit in the car, staring
at the vine's patterns entwined in the fence.
The painting looking at you when you wake.

Gaze down your street — sit up in bed writing
who walks toward you, your hand moving
across the page, catching a dream of children
left alone. The youngest pulled flop-flop along

the sidewalk.

2. Archeology

A painting takes you down the street
on the way to your first school. All the lines
around it, lattice of east and west, north and south.
They teach you those words. You don't know

the street names. The shape of each house,
the Walkers' place (Brenda Walker is your friend).
Here's the Browns', the biggest house is the Pennistons'.
A side door where a teenage girl emerges.

A house with curtains closed. Your house between
the Shaulties and the Parkers. Three paintings on a wall.
A row of galaxies spinning on their own axes. Lines
of a painting press on you, city upon city.

3. Hue

One round instead of gridded, streets gone
to circles and rivers. Your mother's heart grows
large, inflated like a pumpkin. Tubes,
a pole with something dripping. Liquid outside
which should be in. They cut her down the middle,
leave her open.

When you walk down a street, you imagine
finding what it is you need. As if there's another poem,
a better one a few blocks a way, another city's
maze of streets.

Your mother more than
bones, putting on her good coat,
striding down the road to find you —

hue
electric.

Perched where I saw nothing

Bedroom

big bare beautiful emptied

space

curtainless windows full of light

chest shell: drawers gone
mirror
unhinged
what is it
to love each other

it took years to turn naked
toward him: look him full in the face

Species

I am sitting up in bed writing. You come to the door, open it. *Oh, I thought you were downstairs,* you back out, gently drawing the door closed. You don't pull at words, use them extravagantly, or climb into them, reach for them as if they will save you. You make notes on swallows and swifts, sketch warblers and wrens. You tell me, *this hill's covered in asphodel. See the white flower.* You walk slowly, point out the processional caterpillar. Farther down the path, *Look at the length of this centipede.* When I read you a poem, you say nothing — but you can tell me the name of any bird.

Perched where I saw nothing

Twenty-four years after we first leaned toward each other, my husband
asks, *Can I bring you a hot drink?* I never wanted husband, wife

to husband. I wanted lover to lover, Libya, Swaziland. But, yes, I'd love
a lemon and honey. I tried out *my husband* in this poem. What have

all these school lunches, can't get the kids to the table, one meal after
another, done to us? Twenty-four is more than my age when we met.

When I pause in battling our small rooms, I find you studying toucans
of Costa Rica. You take me down the trail to show me owls. Long-Eared

have gone — shy birds, you say. Look: a Snowy distant in that clearing.
Boreals dreaming of voles. At first, I can't see the Saw-whet. Then it appears:

something, where I saw nothing. We lean toward this tiniest owl, round-faced
phantom, watch it watch us.

Labour Day Toronto

I'm supposed to be watching my daughter —
                    last day for the water
slide. Parents shouting at the boys'
                    baseball game. A couple of girls
scratch the dirt beside the stands —
                    popsicle stick

scribbling. Planes circle the lakeshore. Formation of five,
                    dive-bombing trees. Sky-writing.
Swoop of the unsupervised slide.
                    I can't stop

looking up.

Unnaturally warm

for January, more than a thaw. The weather is wrong.
We smile, then grimace. *Eerie,* says my neighbour. *Like March.*

An old woman is raking her lawn. The icebergs are melting. Anything
can happen, and is. We sing off-tune, our plumage

fluorescent.

The budgie lands on my knee

                                                    pecks at the seams
of my jeans, light footsteps down my leg. *Don't eat the fluff*

off my slippers. He walks across my notebook. *That bird's just like me,*
Aunt Ena said on her only visit from Ireland, *always busy, working away*
at something. He jiggled his bell then, gazed at his reflection. Freed

from his cage, he stands on the clock, admires
his big self in the mantelpiece mirror. Turquoise. He flies
from his cage to my head and back.

My father has died and I'm afraid to leave the house.

The warblers wander

Only yesterday I read why the warblers
are disappearing from Germany.
Rosa Luxembourg, 1917

The warblers wander the tree-
tops, far from us dropping ice cream wrappers.

Our hypoallergenic dogs yap at squirrels. Yesterday
Wendy stood in High Park studying a grove of robins over-

wintering, wondering, *Are there more this year?* Early March
brings the wigeons back to Humber Bay. *Make a joyful noise*

unto the Lord. Keening. Le plus-que-parfait doesn't help.
False economies of grammar ransacking hollow trees,

fallow land, thickets and shrubs. *Took all the trees put them*
in a tree museum. Robin's egg blue. Red-winged blackbird

tilts over slashed canvas.

Catch

child on a couch upside-down
legs up the wall   doorframe
    above door
      a small wall to step over

I want to see what I'm seeing
    catch myself perceiving

an outstretched hand   palm open

                    call it grace
something new

catch my throat trying
    to say   this is how it is
this   this   this

as if a word
    is/isn't a story
as if words could

paint the air
    pull colours   shapes
textures   catch senses

claiming a word free

I can hold more than one

poem in my hand, stand up with a fistful,
not worry about them being offended or attacking each other.
Everyone wants something from me, but I am slipping

into repose. I want Greek or Turkish music, lyrics I can't understand.
The more foreign the better. It matters how you enter. Skip the road map.
Here's my compass in its old leather case. See if it works for you.

If you step out your door, the dog will lead you to the park. Step after step.
Do not waver. Let a poem from the beginning speak to one at the end.
Chambers open to each other, one room leads to another. Your belly

has a poem for your busy brow. Hollow in the haiku of your throat.
Toes tapping tankas. The left hand knows what the right wants.
A short fat stanza lunches with a long-lined couplet.

The first and last line tango. All in their varied hats — straw, cloche, tam,
Russian. Their many spectacles — sunglasses, bifocals, pointy Batwoman
frames. Poodles meet Dachshunds. The poem says, enter a trance. Trust me.

Your breath slowing to a word.

How you want to keep saying it

Poetry isn't a theory of anything. It's lonely and afraid. If you love it right, it turns to you, tells you what it needs. Turns right round and looks you in the face. Your breath shallow. Call it map or lover if you like, call it what you will.

You are here only once. You can sit by yourself listening to music. Pat the dog. Look in your daughter's guitar case, lift up all the dog-eared pieces of music, rub your hands over fuchsia velvet, strange and soft: a colour you've never seen.

Laugh at yourself and the dog and the word *dog,* how you want to keep saying it. Look at your daughter's pages called *Guitar Tablature.* Don't know that word: you could say it all day. *Tablature.*

Velvet brush cut, the hair on the back of your first boyfriend's head, before he left to summer in the naval reserve, your fingers brushing, he would stroke your face till you thought he could hold you. Words in the ends of your fingers. You used to fall in love with artists. Now: *Tablature.*

Poetry is the old woman next door still alive in spring, slashing at an overhanging branch of your tree with a rake. It's the way she can lift it over her head, give it a shake. It's her orange sheer covering pink foam curlers.

Poetry is your father's scarf the day after he died, how it was all you wanted. How you were afraid to ask. How you love what they say about tablature in the dictionary, how you believe words help. You place them on a page, give them to someone in an act of faith. How love lunges from noun to verb.

The number of sides to a star

Letters in the alphabet. Shape
of a canvas. How many

poems in a book? Count them. Their
dimensions. Number of women who paint
in a ramble of studios. Ages. Dates

we were born. Shades of green: thousands. The distance
between this studio and home. All the people we have loved.
Fractions. Decimals. Multiplying fantasies. The common
denominator. Blues I have no words for. Points of the compass.

Count of golden flowers on this yellow teacup. The windows
in my house. The weight of joy divided by sadness.
Measure of light. How many friends I need.
Reasons for painting. My heart rate when I look at
this painting. The number of times I

turn to you.

Notes on Poems

In "Two black oaks" the italicized lines are from Jan Zwicky's "Aspen in Wind" from *Robinson's Crossing* (Brick Books, 2004) and appear within the stanza in this form:

> What is the light for
> but to lie down in? What is sorrow for
> but to lie down in.

"Between body and" is a variation on a glosa using words from Margaret Atwood's poem "You Come Back," the first poem in *Morning in the Burned House*. (McClelland & Stewart, 1995.)

"Thule" is inspired by a sculpture at the Ontario Art Gallery, described as *Female Figure*, ivory, 6.1 cm, artist unknown, 300 BC to AD 500, Alaska (Bering Sea or Thule). Thule is pronounced too-lee or thoo-lee. It was written as part of an ekphrastic response to art in the gallery organized by Kelley Aitken in 2009.

"Arterial" was inspired by three of Carolyn Jongeward's paintings, "Above Ground," "Below Ground," and "Shared Ground." (24 inches x 32 inches, acrylic on cloth-covered board).

"The Warblers Wander" was written to resonate with Wendy Weaver's painting *For the Birds* (30 inches x 15 inches, oil on canvas). Rosa Luxemburg's words are from a letter to Sonja Liebknecht, written on May 2, 1917 published in *Letters* (Humanities Press, 1993), pages 202-3. The italicized words in the fifth stanza are from Joni Mitchell's song, "Big Yellow Taxi," 1970.

"The Number of Sides to a Star" was inspired by Carolyn Jongeward's painting "Untitled 1," Mixed Media.

Working with Carolyn Jongeward and Wendy Weaver is part of a collaboration which has taken place over several years between my poetry group, The Long Dash, and the studio painters of the Women's Art Association of Canada.

"Thule" is for Kelley Aitken. "Greenwood" is for Christine Almeida. "Born" is for Michelle and Tristan Meyer. "We write facing the window" is for Noreen Shanahan. "Everyone's father" is for Allison MacDuffee. "November 11th" is for Julie Berry. "A poet I know" is for Ronna Bloom. "Catch" is for Tanya Titchkosky.

About the Author

Sheila Stewart's first collection of poetry, *A Hat to Stop a Train,* was published by Wolsak and Wynn in 2003. She also co-edited *The Art of Poetic Inquiry* (Backalong Books, 2012). Her work has been recognized by numerous literary awards including the GritLit Poetry Competition, Scarborough Arts Council, *Pottersfield Portfolio* Short Poem Competition, Dan Sullivan Memorial Prize, and the Ray Burrell Award for Poetry. She has been widely published in such journals as *The Malahat Review, The Antigonish Review, Grain, Descant,* and *The New Quarterly.*

Stewart grew up in Stratford, Waterloo, and Montreal, taught in Libya and Swaziland, and worked in community-based adult literacy in Parkdale. She lives in Toronto, where she is completing a poetic PhD at the Ontario Institute for Studies in Education of the University of Toronto. She lives with her partner and two daughters near High Park, where she walks her dog.